Jim Thorpe,
the Legend Remembered

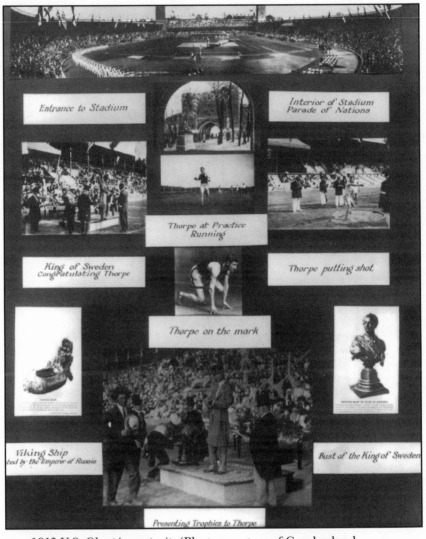

1912 U.S. Olympic composite (Photo courtesy of Cumberland Historical Society, Carlisle, Pennsylvania 17013)

Jim Thorpe

the Legend Remembered

By Rosemary K. Updyke

PELICAN PUBLISHING COMPANY
Gretna 1997

*The word "Pelican" and the depiction of a pelican are trademarks
of Pelican Publishing Company, Inc., and are registered
in the U.S. Patent and Trademark Office.*

Library of Congress Cataloging-in-Publication Data

Updyke, Rosemary K.
    Jim Thorpe, the legend remembered / by Rosemary K. Updyke.
        p.   cm.
    Includes bibliographical references (p.   ).
    Summary: A biography of the American Indian known as one of the
best all-round athletes in history for his accomplishments as an Olympic
medal winner and as an outstanding professional football and baseball
player.
    ISBN 1-56554-212-6 (alk. paper)
    1. Thorpe, Jim, 1887-1953—Juvenile literature. 2. Track and field
athletes—United States—Biography—Juvenile literature. [1. Thorpe, Jim,
1887-1953. 2. Athletes. 3. Indians of North American—Biography.] I.
Title.
GV697.T5U63 1997
796'.092—dc20 —dc20
[B]   96-41488
                                                                              CIP
                                                                               AC

Manufactured in the United States of America
Published by Pelican Publishing Company, Inc.
1101 Monroe Street, Gretna, Louisiana 70053

To Charlotte Thorpe, daughter of James Francis Thorpe, who kindly supported my goal of a book about her father, and, though we never met, offered through cards and letters and phone conversations a warm friendship and genuine inspiration.

To Herbert David "Johnny" Johnston, a superb athlete in his own right, who first introduced me to the legend of the world's greatest athlete.

To my dear husband, Delbert, for his understanding, his unsurpassed patience during the writing of the book, and his daily endeavors to insure its being.

Contents

Introduction:
The Olympic Games

Jim Thorpe, one of the sports stars representing the United States at the 1912 Olympics—held that year in Stockholm, Sweden—still shines, more than eighty years later, in the athletic heavens. Named "the world's greatest athlete," Jim Thorpe today remains an Olympic symbol.

The ancient Olympic Games were first held every four years in Olympia, Greece, beginning in 776 B.C. They were banned by Emperor Theodosius in 393 A.D. Originally only one race, a sprint, constituted the Games, and an olive wreath was the prize for the winner.

With a renewal of the Games in Greece, other races, boxing, and wrestling were added. Even chariot races were included, and more elaborate prizes were awarded.

The idea of the modern Olympics was conceived by Baron Pierre de Coubertin of France in 1892. Intrigued by the idea of a renewal of the Games, he spent nearly three and a half years searching for support for his plans. The strongest interest came from Greece, where the games had begun, and where, it was decided, they should be held again.

In 1896 an International Olympic Committee was established to oversee the Games.

The second modern Olympics were held in de Coubertin's hometown of Paris in 1900. The events, which had now grown in number, were spread out over a period of five months.

For the 1904 Olympics, President Theodore Roosevelt had to choose between Chicago and St. Louis, as both appealed to him for the honor. St. Louis was designated and the Games took place over four and a half months, with some events including only Americans.

The well-planned 1912 Olympics, held in a beautifully constructed new stadium in Stockholm, Sweden, saw the first use of electric timing devices as well as a public address system.

The Olympics scheduled for Berlin in 1916 were canceled because of World War I. In ancient times, wars were suspended so that the Games might go on!

Baron de Coubertin had long ago envisioned a continuance of the games every four years. He had felt that bringing together the youth of all countries periodically for those amicable athletic trials, this bringing of nations closer together, promoting understanding of all cultures, would ensure peace in the world.

Today we hope for a continuance of the Games *forever*!

Jim Thorpe,
the Legend Remembered

CHAPTER 1

Grandfather and Father

Future Olympic superstar Jim Thorpe was born May 28, 1888, in a cabin along the banks of the North Canadian River in Oklahoma. His father was a Sac and Fox Indian and his mother was a Potawatomi.

Jim's grandfather, Hiram G. Thorpe, was an Irish immigrant who settled in Connecticut in the early 1800s. Employed as a blacksmith, he became enticed by stories he heard of the tracking and trapping opportunities offered on the new frontiers, and decided to make the move westward. His new occupation, based primarily in the wilds, eventually led him to settle with a Sac and Fox tribe in the Kansas territory.

Originally the Sac and Fox Indians had lived on the rich-soiled lands near the river valleys of Iowa and western Illinois. Pioneers, streaming westward in increasing numbers, had discovered the lush pastures and had claimed the tribal lands for their own. More and more deadly confrontations occurred as the Indians stoutheartedly resisted. The United States government stepped into the fray with the decision to create a "homeland for all Indians"on the Great Plains of the southwest.

Sac and Fox leader Chief Black Hawk, adamant that tribal lands not be violated, led his people's stand against the growing white influx. Only after thousands of his warriors were

killed in battles known as the Black Hawk War (1831 to 1832)
did he recognize the fact that his tribe was too outnumbered
and outgunned to withstand the continued onslaught.

The resultant treaty required the Sac and Fox tribes to give
up that valuable strip of land along the Mississippi. In return,
they were granted $600,000 which was slated to be paid to
them over the next thirty years. There would be an original
cash sum followed by annuity payments to each family member, along with the provision of certain monthly supplies.

Reluctantly, Black Hawk signed the treaty, which relegated
him and nearly one hundred thousand members of the Sac
and Fox Indian nation to reservation life in Kansas. Hiram
Thorpe learned all of this as he settled onto that Kansas
reservation.

He soon learned, too, that it was not unusual for a pio-
neering man, arriving alone in the west, to take an Indian
woman as a wife. She, being more accustomed than a white
woman to the hardships of wilderness living, could make the
difference in his comfort. She could perhaps even determine
whether or not he could survive in his new lifestyle.

Accordingly, shortly after Hiram's arrival in Kansas, he
took as his bride No-ten-o-quah, a granddaughter of Chief
Black Hawk. The Sac and Fox chief accepted the union,
which was soon blessed with a son.

It was quickly evident that young Hiram P. inherited almost
none of his father's Irish features except for the prominent
jawline. Instead, he bore a remarkable resemblance, with his
jet black hair and bronze-toned skin, to Black Hawk.

Before long it became patently clear to those forced into
the new territory that the Kansas reservation represented a far
from comfortable life. Where they had once been accustomed to cultivating vegetables in the rich soil of the lush
green lands they had lost in the treaty, the Kansas land proved
to be too dusty, too dry, and too hot to produce good crops.

The tribal hunters also soon found that the deer and buffalo herds, formerly a primary source of food, clothing, and
shelter, were being decimated by the whites.

Jim's grandfather, Hiram G. Thorpe (Photo courtesy of Oklahoma Historical Society, Archives and Manuscripts Division, Oklahoma City, Oklahoma)

Jim's grandmother, No-ten-o-quah (Photo courtesy of Oklahoma Historical Society, Archives and Manuscripts Division, Oklahoma City, Oklahoma)

Hiram P., though considered to be a half-breed, was entitled to enrollment in the Indian Agency's reservation school. He would have much preferred the freedom to which he was accustomed, being able to roam and play, learning native skills in the lodges of the tribe's grandfathers, rather than being confined in a school and learning the white man's ways. His father, however, understanding the value of education, insisted that his son receive the Agency schooling.

As young Hiram grew, he displayed more than an inheritance of Chief Black Hawk's looks. He grew tall and strong and showed a tendency toward the chief's legendary athletic prowess. Growing into a muscular young man and displaying a competitive nature, young Hiram Thorpe, like his grandfather before him, was soon recognized as the tribe's best athlete. And, like his native ancestor, he prized the freedom to roam and to live close to nature, and he despised the confines of reservation living.

He had obeyed the Indian Agency restrictions during his school days but once he was home again he submerged himself into the Indian lifestyle. Grown to manhood, Hiram took a Shawnee wife and fathered two daughters and a son. On the harsh, hot, dry land he so despised, he eked out a living for them.

But while the children were still small, he lost his wife to diphtheria. That seemed the final straw. Taking his daughters and four-year-old son, he joined a group of friends in a trek south to the land that would later become Oklahoma.

Shortly after settling into the new territory, Hiram took another wife, Potawatomi/Kickapoo Charlotte View. They built a small cabin along the banks of the North Canadian River where their son George was born. A year later twin girls were born, one living only one year, the other surviving to the age of four.

In 1887, as a result of the General Allotment Act, Thorpe's expanding family received additional annuities along with a 160-acre tract of land. As a result, they were eventually able to move into a larger, more comfortable home farther north along the North Canadian River.

Hiram, content with their new surroundings, cleared the land and raised horses, cattle, hogs, and chickens. Charlotte, meanwhile, cared for a time-consuming garden, raising healthy vegetables to help feed the burgeoning family.

CHAPTER 2

Childhood Days

James Francis Thorpe and his twin brother, Charles, were
born in the new home on May 28, 1888.

Following the tradition of many Indian tribes, Charlotte
sought to recapture a memorable moment occurring just
before the child's birth with an appropriate phrase. This
phrase would be his Indian name. Recalling the serene scene
of sunlight along the path to their house, Jim's mother was
inspired to call him Wa-Tha-Huck, "Bright Path."

Of the two lusty-lunged infants, Charles, with his darker
complexion, had more the appearance of their Indian ances-
try. Jim was lighter skinned and was the only one of the two to
inherit their father's strong Irish jaw.

As youngsters, the boys thrived on the outdoors life. "Summer and winter," Jim would reminisce fondly in later years,
"Charley and I spent as many hours outside every day as possible."

The brothers, though inseparable and best friends, were
intensely competitive. Whether it was a game of catch, follow-
the-leader, or wrestling, it seemed to always begin with a teas-
ing dare from Jim.

"Let's race," he'd say. "You can't catch me!"

Or "I'll hide. You won't be able to find me!"

Or "Let's swim the creek. I'll get to the other side before
you!"

Most of the time Jim was right. Although Charles was forever willing to accept the challenge, Jim, the more muscular of the two, usually proved to be the stronger and faster one.

Hiram was eager to see the boys develop physically and be adaptable to the wilds. So while they were still very young, he undertook their training in the outdoor life. Six feet tall, muscular, and extremely adept in any physical contest, Hiram trained his sons to follow in his footsteps. Together, he and their mother taught the boys of their heritage.

Putting them on horseback early in their childhood, Hiram taught Jim and Charley to ride Indian-style, without need for a saddle, and taught them to fish and hunt. Jim became enthusiastically proficient on all scores by the age of six.

The boys were both always eager to be included in their father's forays throughout the hundreds of acres the Thorpes now owned. Eventually, though, Charley became unable to keep pace with the vigorous lifestyle in which Jim exulted.

Soon it was Jim alone whom Hiram was instructing in tracking and trapping, snaring and stalking. When Jim brought down his first deer, Hiram, pleased with his young son's growing expertise with a rifle, taught him how to dress the catch and get it home.

The boys also were taught that, even for youngsters, life on a farm could not be all fun and games. The twins learned that they were expected to share the duties of feeding the livestock, cleaning the barn, bringing the cows from the pasture for milking, and helping with the planting of crops. Jim, who disliked being inside even for short spans of time, nevertheless realized he must meet his share of responsibilities if he was to be allowed other freedoms.

The reservation's Indian Agency required youngsters to attend school at the age of six. Hiram, remembering his days at school in Kansas, recalled how he also had not wanted to attend but had through the years grown to appreciate the education he had acquired. He was, in fact, one of the few adults on the reservation who could speak English, read, and write. Now he was pleased with the prospect of his sons having the same opportunity.

The twins' older brother, George, was already a student at the agency's mission school. He was faring well now but, having made the drastic change a few years earlier, was able to sympathize with them. Since the school was more than twenty miles away from the Thorpes' farm, Jim and Charley had to board at the school, as George did. That meant that they must live at the school all year except for summer vacations.

The school's dress code put them into unaccustomed heavy wool suits for their daily classes with shirts, ties, shoes, and dark felt hats. Their hair was cut. Their days were regulated by the ringing of bells for waking, for the call to meals, and for the change of classes.

Another of the difficult rules Indian children had to endure was the one forbidding the students to speak their native tongue. They had to learn to read, write, and speak English.

Discipline for any infraction of the rules was harsh and swift, often administered with a wooden paddle or rulers smacked across the knuckles. The total change in lifestyle was difficult and frightening for most of the new young Indian students. For Jim, the confinement inside was perhaps hardest of all to accept. There was never again an opportunity for him to drift off into the woods for an hour (or a day, as Jim often had back on the farm).

Half of the school day was spent teaching reading, writing, and the basics of arithmetic. The other half was devoted to industrial training for the older students and small chores about the school for younger ones.

Charley, his teachers agreed, was the more adaptable of the twins. Jim was inclined to be restless, less attentive, and less responsive to the rules. Most of the students were intimidated by the changes the school brought into their lives. They, too, chafed at the previously unknown restrictions. But it was Jim who totally balked. He ran away from school!

Finding his way back home was no problem for the outdoor-oriented Jim. But a problem arose when Hiram looked out of the window and saw his son walking across the yard toward the house.

He understood immediately that Jim was delinquent from the school and reacted swiftly, with a lesson of his own. Jim quickly learned that the discipline he had encountered in school was minimal compared to what he could expect at the hand of his angered father.

"Jim, you are going back!" Hiram told him emphatically. "You have the opportunity for an education, a chance to better yourself! You are going back there and *learn!*"

Hiram put Jim into the open cart again and took the sulking boy back to school.

To make his following days there more endurable, Jim learned to immerse himself in games during free time. The friendly competition, keeping his mind and body active, helped overshadow his unhappiness.

During summer vacations from school, Jim continued to help his father around the farm. Hiram, hoping to help Jim work off a bit of his bottled-up energies, began training him in the breaking of some of the smaller horses Hiram now raised. The combativeness of the horse's spirit against Jim's was exciting to the youngster.

By the time he was eight or nine years old, Jim had progressed to camping alone and grew to look forward all the more to summer vacations from the school. Eventually, as Jim became more and more adept with a rifle, Hiram approved all-night camping alone with one of the Thorpes' hunting dogs for company.

Back at school for his third year, Jim remained lax in his attitude, but his teachers reported that he was showing better progress in his grades. Then, in the spring of that year, an epidemic struck the school and Charley became ill with smallpox. Pneumonia added to his complications and young Charles died at the age of eight.

Jim, devastated by the loss of his brother, his best friend, sank into a deep depression that no one and nothing could shake from his young shoulders. Feeling that he simply could not face returning to school, he sought his father out in the barn one day and begged to be allowed to stay home and work on the farm.

"I can help with the chores," he pleaded. "You know I can take care of feeding the animals! And keeping the barn clean! I'll do more! I'll . . . "

Hiram put aside the saw he had been sharpening and turned to his desperate young son, motioning him to sit down.

"First of all," he explained with unusual patience, "you know that there is an agency ruling about education for children on the reservation and for that reason alone, you must stay in school." He went on to relate how he felt about the importance of education, and how Jim would also, as he grew older.

Downhearted in his failure to get his father's consent, Jim agreed to try again.

But by the middle of the term, without permission, Jim was home again, once more trying to convince his father that he was old enough and strong enough and competent enough to help about the farm.

This time Hiram lost all patience and told Jim in no uncertain terms that he would return to school, even if he had to be sent so far away that he couldn't walk home again.

CHAPTER 3

Haskell Institute, Kansas

Jim soon learned that it had not been an idle threat when his father had told him he would like to send him to a school so far away he couldn't possibly find his way back. Jim remembered those words distinctly as the two began a long wagon ride, the first step of a very long trip toward the new school where his father had enrolled him.

Eleven-year-old Jim was put aboard a train traveling north to just beyond the Kansas state line. Then he transferred to another train that took him to Lawrence, a few miles west of Kansas City, where the Haskell Institute was located.

Although intrigued by his first train ride, Jim had sat glumly, eyes glued to the window. By the time he finally arrived at the school, he felt certain he had counted off each one of the entire three hundred miles he had traveled.

He was met at the station in Kansas City and taken to the school. From first glance he was impressed by its grand appearance. Though he sat quietly, his eyes recorded the school's impressive entrance as they passed beneath an arch that proclaimed the school's name. Beyond that, the school's main street wove past beautiful stone buildings, the dormitories, faculty homes, and the administration building.

Once officially signed in, Jim was immediately introduced to the school's obligatory rules and regulations.

Haskell, he found, operated on themes of classroom education and military discipline. The nearly six hundred students were provided with manual training in either the wagon shop which produced wagons, the tailor shop which manufactured uniforms, the bakery, or the farm.

Students marched to every daily event, row upon row of young scholars. Throughout the day, bells would send them into their classrooms, to lunch; the bells regulated their every waking hour.

They were to be responded to promptly, assuring precise arrival and departure to and from every scheduled event of the day. Harsh, swift discipline ensured that no one lagged behind.

As in the agency's mission school, at Haskell the student's own Indian language was forbidden. There was also a dress code to contend with; uniform and cap were obligatory.

Once again Thorpe settled into a detested school routine. His attitude and aptitude ratings remained on a passing level. He coasted along, keeping to himself, staying in the background as much as possible. However, he did appear to be faring a little better in his studies than he had in the agency school.

Although baseball was Haskell's main sport, Jim was more intrigued with football. He had never even held one until one of the school's young football stars, noticing his interest, made him a ball of sewed leather straps filled with rags. With it, Jim organized a team of boys his age for some fun-filled recreational hours. They would imitate plays that they watched the Haskell team practicing on the football field.

For the first time, Jim seemed to be coming out, at least during free time, of the lonely shell he had built around himself ever since his brother's death. His teachers began to notice an improvement in both the classroom and in manual training.

For nearly two years Jim maintained that improvement. Then suddenly he was faced with the need to get back home again despite the miles. During lunch, one of his classmates sought him out, whispering, "Jim, I just heard in the office that your father has been shot and may be dying!"

"What?" Jim gasped. "What happened?"

"I don't know," the boy replied. "I was just leaving the office when I heard . . . "

But Jim didn't wait for more. Without checking with the office, without seeking permission, and without stopping to pack a bag of clothing, he dashed off the premises, heading for the railroad yard in hopes of snagging a ride back home on a freight train.

He arrived at the freight yard just as one train, engine puffing smoke, prepared to pull out. Leaping in the open door of a freight car, he rolled over to a corner and huddled out of sight until the train was out of town and gaining speed. His thoughts were riveted on his injured father. Can I make it in time? his mind cried over and over during the following hours.

Just at dusk the train slowed and pulled over to a water tower. Not wanting to chance being seen by railroad men and thrown off the train, Jim crept cautiously to the door and peered out. Suddenly his heart leapt into his throat. In his panic his father's teaching of directions had been forgotten. Jim had hopped a freight going north, not south toward Oklahoma and the Thorpe ranch! Hours had been lost while the train had traveled in the opposite direction of the one he wanted.

It took almost two weeks for Jim to reach home; he had to walk much of the way. Road-weary but relieved, he finally stumbled into the Thorpe yard and was met by his incredulous father who had, thankfully, recovered.

Though angry and disappointed that Jim had left school without permission or even finding out if the trip was really necessary, his father was nonetheless grateful for his son's concern and didn't send him back right away.

Within a few short weeks, another tragedy struck when Jim's mother was stricken with blood poisoning and died. Again, death devastated the youngster.

This time, Hiram decided not to return Jim to Haskell but to enroll him instead in the local public school, letting Jim help on the ranch during the next four years.

Once again Jim became immersed in sports, fitting them in between chores on the ranch and schooling. Since there were no football teams in the area, Jim settled for baseball, pitching for the local team.

It was during his third year in the school that a recruiter from the Carlisle Indian School in Pennsylvania visited. Jim had been privileged to see the Carlisle football team once while he was enrolled at Haskell, and now, with the school seeking recruits, Jim wanted desperately to go there.

His father was delighted with Jim's decision. Once more he sent his son on a long journey to school.

CHAPTER 4

The Carlisle Indian School

Quite a different Jim Thorpe left home early in February for a school half a continent away. This time, going to school was Jim's choice.

Although he was notably nervous, anticipation outweighed apprehension. Sixteen-year-old Jim, train ticket in hand, began the journey that would make a profound change in his life.

Having seen the Carlisle football team once when they visited the Haskell school, and having heard of their exploits, Jim was willing to follow strict rules for an opportunity to play on the Indian team.

His arrival in Pennsylvania in the middle of winter found the school's landscape lightly covered with snow, enhancing the broad, tree-lined parade ground. Facing it on both sides were two- and three-storied wooden structures with dormitories, classrooms, workshops, and school offices. The site had originally been a fort which was burned during the Civil War.

The Carlisle Indian School was the culmination of the dream of the school's founder, army officer Colonel Richard Henry Pratt. Following the Civil War, Pratt, who served as a white officer with a black regiment known as Buffalo Soldiers, had acquired a distinct sympathy for the minority group.

Richard Henry Pratt, Superintendent of Carlisle Indian School, 1879-1904 (Photo courtesy of Cumberland County Historical Society, Carlisle, Pennsylvania 17013)

Jim Thorpe as student at Carlisle Indian School (Photo courtesy of Oklahoma Historical Society, Archives and Manuscripts Division, Oklahoma City, Oklahoma)

The Carlisle youngsters soon found that Warner could be a tough taskmaster, but they were willing to give their all in an effort to meet his criteria. They understood that he was trying to make winners of them. And make winners, he did!

When he discovered Jim Thorpe, he knew the young Indian would also one day be a winner. But not even Pop Warner could visualize how much of a winner the young man would become.

CHAPTER 5

Jim and Varsity Football

Jim's path toward making the varsity football team took numerous twists and turns during his first years at Carlisle. At first his dreams were on hold, but he had chosen what he wanted and was determined to stay with it until his dream was realized.

Teachers at Carlisle remarked on how well he was doing, compared to what they had heard of his attitude at other schools. His grades showed a decided improvement. Jim was determined now.

He had a goal.

Despite his change for the better, personal bad luck continued to stalk him. Jim had only been enrolled in Carlisle a few months when he received the news that his father had died of blood poisoning. Because of the distance between school and home, Jim was unable to attend the funeral. With his father's loss, Jim was again severely depressed.

He was due to be assigned soon to an outing. It was decided, in light of his recent tragedy, that it might be beneficial to put him in the midst of family life right away. However, instead of an outing with outdoors activities, which Jim would have preferred, he found himself cleaning indoors. Eventually even the family he was living with realized he was not cut out for the assignment, and he was transferred to a farm in New Jersey, where he found the work much more compatible.

Little by little Jim was able to overcome the deep depression that the latest fatality in his family had caused. By the time he returned to school at summer's end, now nineteen years old, he showed an even more outgoing attitude than before.

That was the young man "Pop" Warner first encountered, quite by accident. In later years Jim would relate the incident with a sly grin at the remembrance.

He had been walking through the stadium one afternoon after class, Jim said, when he noticed the varsity track team working out on the field and stopped to watch their high jump practice from the sidelines. One after another of the team failed to clear the bar which was set for five feet, nine inches. Intrigued, Jim finally felt impelled to ask if he might take a turn.

Although the boys were quietly laughing at him, ridiculing his assumption that he could come anywhere near their practiced efforts, they stood aside to watch his attempt. And even though he was hardly dressed for track competition, Jim easily cleared the bar, then trotted off with a wave and a thank you, leaving behind a surprised audience of young athletes staring after him.

Word of the incident quickly reached the coach, who summoned Jim into his office early the next morning. As was his habit, Jim began the conversation with an apology; he didn't know for what, but he thought that being called into the office had to mean he had done something wrong.

"No, no," Warner hurriedly assured him. "I wanted to talk to you about the way you cleared the bar at track practice yesterday."

"Oh, that," Jim replied offhandedly. "I probably could have done better if I'd had on track shoes and been dressed for practice."

As a result of that unplanned show of ability, Warner immediately made Jim a member of the track team. Soon, the shy young Indian was starring in track events for Carlisle. In one, he won both the high jump and the 120-yard high hurdles, and came in second in the 220-yard dash. He continued to perform in that way at subsequent track meets, becoming a name to be reckoned with. Warner watched, impressed with Jim's dedication and his determination to win any event in which he participated.

But Jim was not content with his new celebrity status. He still wanted to play football and continued to badger Warner every chance he got. Exasperated, the coach tried over and over again to explain to Jim that he was an important part of the track team now and that Warner didn't want his new star getting hurt in such a rough-and-tumble game as football.

Recognizing his coach's concern and realizing that he was lucky to at least be on a Carlisle team, Jim continued to hone his skills in track. He practiced faithfully and gave his all at the meets. But every so often, he would momentarily forget his new resolution and once again plague Warner with pleas to play football.

Finally, with summer drawing to a close and football practice on the agenda again, Warner gave in to the extent of allowing Jim to join tackle practice. Elated, Jim suited up and joined the team on the field.

Again he exasperated his coach, who nonetheless watched in admiration as Jim took the ball and raced toward the goal, outstripping the entire practice team. "Jim," Warner yelled after him as Jim raced down the field, "you aren't supposed to run *through* the team! You're supposed to be giving the guys practice tackling *you!*"

Warner would long remember Jim's reply, and repeat it many times in later years, describing Jim's determination. "*Nobody* tackles Jim!" Thorpe replied.

Warner had thrown up his hands at that, muttering to himself about the hard-headedness of the youth. But it was not a mere boast he'd heard that day. Whenever he gave Jim the opportunity to run the ball, Jim continued to leave the team behind.

The coach could clearly see that he was watching a youngster with ability and dedication, and moved the elated Jim Thorpe onto his varsity squad.

CHAPTER 6

The Carlisle Indian Teams

Pop Warner had coached the Carlisle Indians to many winning games, but he declared that their 1907 football team was "about the most perfect" he had ever sent onto the field up until that time. They ended the season with a streak of ten victories.

Jim Thorpe did little to add to the team's prestige in the early part of that football season, as Warner kept the fledgling player benched during the first games to give him the opportunity to learn the techniques and technicalities of the game. Feeling that Jim was not big enough yet, but seeing his potential, Warner put him under the expert guidance of Albert Exendine, one of Carlisle's young track and field stars.

Jim was eagerly awaiting the opportunity to play, and was disappointed to have been put "on hold," but he set his powers of observation on each play, learning the whys and wherefores of the game. It was late in the season before he got his first taste of playing in a big game, when Warner signaled him in to replace an injured halfback.

Jim still had nearly a year to wait before he could start making the spectacular plays that would one day become his trademark.

He continued to practice with the varsity track team, where his love of competition had an opportunity to pour forth.

When track season opened, he represented Carlisle flawlessly. He was often paired with Louis Tewanima, a young Hopi Indian, on trips to compete at other schools. Both Jim and Louis were among the stars Warner took to the Penn Relays. There, Thorpe's stunning six feet, one inch high jump won him a gold medal. Throughout that season, he continued dominating every track event in which he was entered.

Even with his new fame, Jim was nonchalant about the records he racked up, being far more concerned with the winning itself.

Soon it seemed that those wins had empowered Jim to overcome his past problems in the classroom. Confidence began to take the place of anxiety. In both his academic and personal lives, this soon became noticeable to his peers and his teachers.

It was not until the following football season that Thorpe's name would become widely recognized. Carlisle began to encounter more prestigious contenders, big names such as Penn State, Syracuse, and the University of Pennsylvania. And the Indians began to dominate these teams. Harvard was added to their list of opponents, as well as the University of St. Louis and the University of Denver (who were Rocky Mountain Conference champions). Carlisle, with Jim running, kicking, and passing, ended the 1908 season with ten wins, two losses and one tie. All of the records set were due in large part to Thorpe's plays, beating opponents with a total of 212 points to their 55.

Then, crowning Jim's first season as starting halfback, came the momentous announcement that Jim had been named as third-team All American!

With his place on the Carlisle football team secure, Jim happily maintained a hand in other sports as well—even playing some basketball—although track remained his second favorite team sport. The 1909 track season started with a soon-to-be routine performance for Thorpe, as he dominated the Lafayette meet with six gold medals and one bronze.

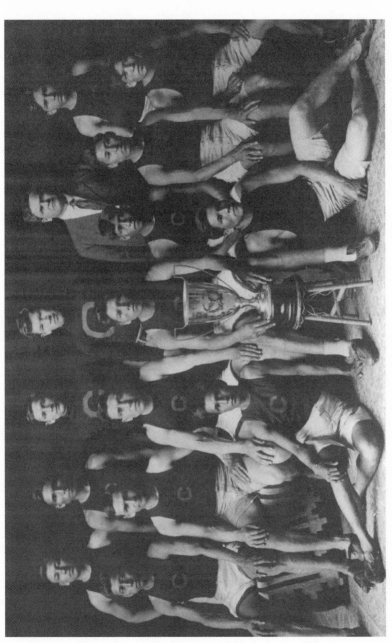

Carlisle Indian School 1909 track team with State Championship cup (Photo courtesy of Cumberland County Historical Society, Carlisle, Pennsylvania 17013)

Having become the school's star athlete, his name and face admired by the entire Carlisle student body, Jim found he was also attracting the attention of his female classmates. He learned to dance, found he liked it, and quickly added that to the list of activities at which he excelled. It was about that time that he became aware of Iva Miller, a very attractive young honor student who would be graduating soon. They began dating.

Also as a result of his star status, and his resulting need to be available at any time for his sports responsibilities, it became possible for Jim to skip some of his former responsibilities, such as the outings.

With no outing scheduled for that summer, Jim for the first time found himself on his own. It was a major change for a young man who had been tied to school schedules ever since he was a six-year-old.

It was then that Jim remembered having heard, through teammates and others, that North Carolina's Rocky Mountain minor-league baseball team sometimes hired college students to play during summer vacations. Sports-loving Jim headed south, deciding to try out for a season with them. He had no problem getting signed on as a third baseman. The few dollars a week he earned went toward his expenses of food and lodging and helped him through the summer. As the season progressed, and the league realized his potential, the coach occasionally started Jim at first base. As they became aware of his pitching strength, they also used Jim in that position.

When the fall term at Carlisle began, Jim did not return to school; he stayed on with the East Carolina League. Two years later, when the league began to wind down, Jim headed back to Oklahoma. He visited with relatives and again experienced long hours in the wild, hunting and fishing, with the old remembered contentment.

It was there that one of his former Carlisle classmates met him quite by accident, in town one day. Witnessing the lethargic difference from the outgoing Thorpe he had gotten to

Iva Miller (Photo courtesy of Oklahoma Historical Society,
Archives and Manuscripts Division, Oklahoma City, Oklahoma)

know at Carlisle, he suggested that Jim should come back to school. Jim, characteristically demeaning his worth, replied that he felt he wouldn't be wanted there anymore.

"Nonsense, Jim!" his friend said. "The team needs you!" At that he saw the old spark in Jim's eyes but could feel Jim's hesitancy to take the first step. Unknown to Thorpe, upon his return to Carlisle, the friend reported the conversation to Warner. A short while later, Jim received a call from the coach, encouraging his return to school. He even proposed training Jim for the upcoming 1912 Olympic Games!

An elated Jim was once again on the Carlisle roster. He quickly fell back into the spirit of the school's athletics, seemingly having lost none of his former expertise. His punting and passing as sharp as ever, Jim now gained national attention in his position as halfback.

Once the football season was past, he turned his attention to basketball while quietly anticipating the day he could begin training for the Olympics as Warner had promised.

True to his intentions, Warner did start Jim on a training program for the Olympics, which were to be held in Sweden. With that goal now on his horizon, Jim continued collecting gold medals as the Carlisle track team moved through their season.

When the regular track season ended late in May, Pop Warner started to ready the young Indians he had chosen as the school's representatives for the trip to the Olympics.

CHAPTER 7

Traveling to the Olympics

It was warm that Friday morning, June 14, 1912, when Carlisle's athletic contingent boarded the SS *Finland* in New York City's harbor. The ship had been especially commissioned to carry all of the U.S. Olympic team members to Stockholm, Sweden, for competition in the fifth Olympiad, scheduled to begin July 6.

Coach Pop Warner ushered the two young Carlisle Indians who had won a place on the Olympic team onto the ship. With a paternal smile, he stood aside and watched the awed reactions of Louis Tewanima and Jim Thorpe to the start of their shipboard journey. Once the boys had checked into their cabins and stored their luggage, they set about acquainting themselves with their new surroundings.

Jim was enthralled. He kept remarking on the "size of the ship!" and the "comfort!" their cabins offered. In the years to come, as he recounted the journey to others, he would continue to describe the SS *Finland* just as enthusiastically as he had that day.

At 9:00 A.M., as the ship prepared to leave the harbor, the Carlisle team joined the other Olympic athletes lining the ship's railing to wave to the crowd of flag-waving well-wishers on the dock.

By that time the next morning, and every morning thereafter on their trip across the ocean, the athletes were

Jim Thorpe, running practice lap on the ship (Photo courtesy of University Archives, John R. Case papers, Urbana, Illinois)

expected to be on deck to train. Cork padding had been laid out around the deck for track practice, with mats in place for vaulting and high jump practice. Daily, Thorpe could be seen jogging conscientiously, winding down after the practice sessions.

Long after the Olympic Games, stories would circulate that insisted that Thorpe had disregarded regulations by skipping practice sessions and lolling about the deck or drinking in his cabin instead. Sports writer Grantland Rice was one of those who perpetuated the story of skipped training. His report was debunked by, among others, Olympic competitor Avery Brundage. Through the years other teammates as well would ridicule those who sparked the idea of Jim's laziness, insisting that Jim was always there "on the mark."

After leaving New York for Stockholm, the SS *Finland* made a scheduled stop in Antwerp, Belgium, where the athletes had three days of arduous training on dry land.

Upon their arrival in Sweden, the visiting athletes were overwhelmed by almost as much enthusiasm and warmth as they had experienced upon their departure from New York's harbor. The team members were treated to tours of Stockholm, acquainting them with the city and its people.

U.S. delegation marching into Olympic Stadium in Stockholm (Photo courtesy of University Archives, John R. Case papers, Urbana, Illinois)

CHAPTER 8

The Games Begin!

On July 6, the long-anticipated 1912 Olympic Games were opened by King Gustav V, whose country was hosting this fifth modern Olympiad.

It was a jubilant occasion as teams from twenty-eight nations marched through the main gateway of the city's beautiful new stadium. The stirring strains of "A Mighty Fortress Is Our God" wafted over audience and contestants as the competing athletes strode in along the cinder path. Among America's Olympic hopefuls marched Jim Thorpe and Louis Tewanima, the two young competitors from the Carlisle Indian School. Each contingent marched smartly behind the flowing flag of their country. As they passed the royal enclosure, they paid their respects to King Gustav, Prince Gustav Adolph, and Grand Duke Dimitri of Russia.

The hosts gave welcoming speeches. And then, the Games were declared open!

The following day, more than twenty thousand sports enthusiasts filled the newly created double-decker Olympic Stadium. Europeans in the audience had arrived at the Olympics feeling certain that their Scandinavian sprint stars would easily capture the track titles.

Instead, they watched in awe as American athlete Jim Thorpe dominated the games after diving enthusiastically into the grueling five-event pentathlon. He won the broad jump and the 200-meter dash, as well as the discus throw. He lost only one match, to Sweden's Hugo Wieslander in the throw of the javelin.

For the fifth event, Jim had drawn an unfortunate starting slot, positioning him in the next-to-outside lane. As a result, Ferdinand Bie of Norway and Avery Brundage of the United States became the favored contenders.

Jim, dressed in his track uniform of white shorts with a shield-emblazoned white top, took his place at the starting line. Planting the toe of his left shoe firmly on his mark, his right foot spaced back for the push-off, he waited. Outwardly calm, he peered along the imposing stretch of track that lay before him.

In his mind's eye he could clearly see his father's face; he could just as easily hear Hiram's voice. Whether it concerned Jim's school grades, or games with friends—whatever Jim attempted—his father had always urged him to do his best. "Always remember," he would say, impressing Jim with pride in his heritage, "you are an Indian. Show them what an Indian can do!" Recalling the words, Jim imperceptibly nodded agreement as he stood ready for the race.

Anticipation heightened in the stands as fans watched the contenders take their places at the starting line, poised and ready. For each of the seven, it was an awesome moment.

Then the starting shot rang out.

Unlike Thorpe, who cantered off from an unexpectedly slow start, his teammate Brundage and Norway's Bie burst forth in the predicted struggle for the lead. Elbows close to their sides, the two churned off to a fast pace, rounding the track in the first lap.

Thorpe, meanwhile, continued to run farther back in the pack than expected. Keenly aware of his position, he studiously paced himself, all the while assessing his competitors. The seven were well into the second lap when Brundage began slowing noticeably. The Norwegian, Bie, immediately seized the lead.

Thorpe realized that that was the moment he must make his

move. Accelerating his pace, he began to move steadily past one contender after another. Sports fans in the stadium were on their feet, breaths held in anticipation as they watched Thorpe, in the third lap, continue that burst of speed and close the gap. Then he breezed past Bie, flinging himself across the finish line several yards ahead of the nearest runner.

Deafening cheers from the crowd poured forth for the American who had proved himself a winner that day with his feats of unequaled speed, endurance, and ability.

A week later, the arduous ten-event decathlon was scheduled, with the contestants facing off on Saturday, July 13. Torrents of rain drenched the participants as well as the onlookers in the stands. While the viewers scampered for cover or huddled under umbrellas, the athletes contended with wet track conditions that led to several sloppy take-offs.

The competition that day had begun with the 100-meter dash which was won by E. R. L. Mercer, who caught Thorpe at the wire. In the running broad jump, Jim faulted twice in the wet take-offs. His third attempt still failed to measure up to that of C. Lomberg of Sweden. With the shot put, however, Thorpe's attempt was sufficient to best competitor Wieslander by two and a half feet.

Both the contestants and their audience in the stands were delighted to see the following day dawn clear and dry, with the track in good condition again. Jim easily took the running high jump with a leap of six feet, one inch, but in the following 400-meter run he trailed Mercer once again.

Racing through the 100-meter hurdles, however, Jim came in with a time of 15.6 seconds, setting a new record that would stand for decades to come. And he forged ahead once again in the 1500-meter run, bettering his pentathlon time by four seconds.

While Thorpe was capturing records in his events, his Carlisle teammate, Louis Tewanima, was also making a name for himself. With Jim lustily cheering him on from the sidelines, Tewanima took second place in the strenuous 10,000-meter race. This earned him an Olympic silver medal.

Jim Thorpe putting shot at 1912 Olympics (Photo courtesy of Cumberland Historical Society, Carlisle, Pennsylvania 17013)

Beginning of the 1500-meter run in decathlon at 1912 Olympics (Photo courtesy of University Archives, Avery Brundage Collection, Urbana, Illinois)

Because of so many other events on the day's schedule, the Games had to be extended one more day, during which Jim placed second in the discus throw, third in the pole vault, and third with the javelin.

Thorpe, who always strove to win at anything he attempted, was dissatisfied with his showing that day. But when the judges huddled to total the scores, American Jim Thorpe was found to have captured an incredible 8,412.96 points out of a possible 10,000! Scoring nearest to Thorpe's total was Sweden's Hugo Wieslander with 7,724 points.

In the afternoon, before a stadium filled with cheering fans, Thorpe was called to the carpeted victory podium. King Gustav placed a laurel wreath upon Jim's head and presented him with a gold medal for his pentathlon win. In addition, the king presented a life-sized bust of himself, measuring four feet by twenty-two inches, to the surprised young athlete.

Later, Thorpe was called to the podium to receive his second gold medal and laurel wreath. This time the king also

Jim Thorpe receiving trophies from King Gustav V of Sweden, 1912 Olympics (Photo courtesy of Cumberland Historical Society, Carlisle, Pennsylvania 17013)

THE WHITE HOUSE
WASHINGTON

July 29, 1912.

My dear Sir:

I have much pleasure in congratulating you on
account of your noteworthy victory at the Olympic
Games in Stockholm.   Your performance is one of
which you may well be proud.   You have set a high
standard of physical development which is only at-
tained by right living and right thinking, and your
victory will serve as an incentive to all to improve
those qualities which characterize the best type of
American citizen.

It is my earnest wish that the future will bring
you success in your chosen field of endeavor.

With heartiest congratulations, I am,

Sincerely yours,

[signature]

Mr. James Thorpe,
    Carlisle, Pennsylvania.

Copy of letter to Thorpe from President Taft (Courtesy of Cumberland
Historical Society, Carlisle, Pennsylvania 17013)

presented him with a gift from the czar of Russia, a spectacular two-foot-long, eighteen-inch-high chalice weighing thirty
pounds, lined with gold and embedded with precious jewels
and formed in the shape of a Viking ship.

As the king enthusiastically shook Thorpe's hand that second time, he made an emotional declaration with words that
would forever after be connected with Jim Thorpe. "Sir," he
said, "you are the greatest athlete in the world!"

The young American, who had set Olympic records that
would be unequaled for many years to come, replied quietly
in his usual modest way, "Thanks, King."

Yes, Jim Thorpe's father would have been proud of the son
who had come to Sweden to represent America, had done his
best, and had come away a winner—not just in the record
books but also in the hearts of those who had witnessed his
performance.

Congratulations for Jim's Olympic wins poured in from
all across the world, including a letter from the President of
United States, William H. Taft, expressing high praise for
Jim's performance and wishing him a successful future.

Back home in the States, fellow Americans were eager to
extend their own honors and show their appreciation to the
hero of the Games. Thorpe's return to the States was delayed,
however, while he and Tewanima visited other European
cities where they had been invited to appear and compete in
post-Olympic games.

It was August before the trio of winning athletes and coach
were finally able to accept the "home grown" accolades back
in the United States. On August 15 they arrived back in
Carlisle, stepping off the train to the accompaniment of
cheers, music, and heartfelt speeches.

In the parade, Thorpe and Tewanima rode in a handsome
horse-drawn carriage, led and followed by band units. After
the town hosted a dinner in their honor that evening, students led the athletes away to a school dance in honor of the
returned heroes.

Victory parade for Thorpe and Tewanima in Carlisle after 1912 Olympics (Photo courtesy of Cumberland County Historical Society, Carlisle, Pennsylvania 17013)

A week later New York City claimed the Olympic winners for a day of celebration, hosting a parade, a theatre party, and a banquet. In the parade, Thorpe rode alone in an open car, vigorously cheered by a throng estimated at a million who shouted his name as he rode past. In his usual modest manner, Thorpe gasped in honest awe, "I never knew one person could have so many *friends!*"

Jim, Pop Warner, and members of the Carlisle football team (Photo courtesy of Oklahoma Historical Society, Archives and Manuscripts Division, Oklahoma City, Oklahoma)

CHAPTER 9

Back to Football

After many celebrations, relative quiet finally returned to Jim's life. Then he was faced with the big decision of whether to go into a career in baseball (he had received a lucrative offer) or return to school.

Football remained his first love in sports, so when Pop Warner suggested Jim return to Carlisle for another year on their team, he grasped at the opportunity. Jim realized, too, that with another year at Carlisle he could earn his certificate of learning; and he had never forgotten the importance his father had attached to education. That was the deciding factor; the question was answered.

Carlisle, though a vocational academic high school, was of collegiate rank in athletics and therefore played against well-known colleges.

To start the 1912 season, Carlisle quickly aced their first four competitors: Albright, Lebanon Valley, Dickinson, and Villanova. They beat Villanova 65-0. With Thorpe now even more a drawing card, stadiums were filled to overflowing any time his name appeared on the roster.

Washington and Jefferson University was not all that easy to beat; Carlisle came away with a 0-0 tie. A week later, Carlisle took the field with an opponent who had beaten the Indians the year before, so there was extra incentive on that rainy day to play their hardest. Thorpe, though notably never happy with athletics in the rain, got three touchdowns on the soggy field.

Later, in quick succession, Carlisle defeated Pitt 45-8 and Georgetown University 34-20. In a game against West Point the Indians completely outplayed the Army with a 27-6 win. After the game, a young cadet who had played guard that day spoke with great admiration of Thorpe's prowess on the football field. That young cadet, who would later become a five-star general and then president of the United States, was Dwight D. Eisenhower. He would repeat emphatically, even years later, his assertion that "on the football field, there was no one like Thorpe in the world. He dominated the game!"

The final game of the season was the traditional Thanksgiving Day bout with Brown University. Jim, realizing that this was a big game for him and his last for Pop Warner, since he would get his college diploma before the next season, was determined to give it all he had. The score was Carlisle 32, Brown 0; Thorpe's season scoring had reached a hefty 198 points. This set an all-time college record for a season point total.

Newspapers from coast to coast carried headlines about him.

Jim headed back to Oklahoma for a Christmas visit with his family.

He returned to Carlisle in early January, just in time to take part in a school dance. As surefooted on the dance floor as he was on the ball field, Jim enjoyed some lighthearted moments dancing with his friends in the school gym. Little did he or the other students know, those would be his last lighthearted moments for quite a while.

CHAPTER 10

The Story Breaks

In January 1913, quite a different kind of story about Jim Thorpe hit the headlines of newspapers across the nation. The reporter who broke the story had stumbled across it the previous year, following Carlisle's game with a small college in Massachusetts.

During a practice session Roy Johnson, a young reporter, latched onto Charley Clancy, a baseball man, for an interview. While they were talking, Clancy did a double-take as Jim trotted by a little way from where they stood. He exclaimed, "He played ball for me one summer!"

Clancy was excited to see young Thorpe again, this time in a football uniform. He recounted to Johnson how he had managed a baseball team a few years earlier and had acquired Jim as a pitcher in a trade. Johnson listened, openmouthed. He was well aware that college students often earned money during the summers by playing baseball. But since they knew that playing professional sports could keep them from playing college sports, they usually used assumed names. An amateur standing was necessary to be eligible for college-level play.

It was also necessary for the Olympics. But here was an Olympic champion, supposed to be an amateur, who was reputed to have earned pro money before taking part in the Games!

For some reason, Johnson didn't write the story right away. He waited until January, when he printed in the Wocester *Telegram* that Jim had played professional baseball for two seasons with a North Carolina ball club.

Thorpe was puzzled when he was called into the school superintendent's office and confronted by a noticeably upset Superintendent Friedman and Pop Warner. Questioned, Jim readily admitted that he had played on the pro team to the aghast duo. He related how he had tagged along with several students from various other schools and signed on to play ball for enough pay to cover his needs for the summer. He had been completely unaware that it could in any way change his amateur status.

Jim was innocent of having played under an assumed name to cover the violation. He had not, since he hadn't known it was a violation.

Warner quickly latched onto Thorpe's suggestion that he would apologize to the Amateur Athletic Union Board, and Friedman agreed. A letter was sent to the board, with Jim explaining that he had broken the rule in all innocence, and begging the board's forgiveness.

The AAU board members, astounded to learn of the situation, promptly called for a hearing to discuss the charges. They warned that if Thorpe was found guilty, his Olympic records would be deleted from the books and he would have to return his medals immediately.

Embarrassed for having allowed Thorpe to take part in the competition, the AAU, in turn, apologized to the International Olympic Committee. The IOC met to discuss the affair and voted to demand the return of the gold medals Thorpe had won for the decathlon and pentathlon, as well as the trophies he had been presented.

When informed of the IOC's decision, Jim was confused and embarrassed. Warner, witnessing his young player's stricken demeanor, and aware that Thorpe was not guilty of planned cheating, helped him pack and ship the medals and trophies back to Sweden.

The public was almost unanimous in its sympathy for Thorpe and declared that he should not have been punished for his mistake. His admission that he hadn't been aware he was breaking the rules was enough for his fans. They believed him and they suffered with him and for him.

The fans' reaction to Jim's humiliation was a great boost to his morale. He was especially appreciative of the response of Norway's Bie and Sweden's Wieslander, the Olympic runners-up, who refused to accept the medals they were offered now that Thorpe's title had been forfeited. Bie and Wieslander stated that they did not feel they had earned them. "Thorpe did!" they both contended.

Thorpe's name was nevertheless stripped from the Olympic records.

But all who saw Jim Thorpe perform during the 1912 Olympics continued to remember him for the outstanding athlete that he was. He would forever be considered what the king had proclaimed him that day: "the greatest athlete in the world!"

Jim Thorpe and Iva Miller's wedding (Photo courtesy of Cumberland County Historical Society, Carlisle, Pennsylvania 17013)

CHAPTER 11

Professional Days Begin

It was time for Jim to put the past behind him and concentrate on the future. He debated the wisdom of which lane to take next.

There were several options. A few major-league baseball teams had come bidding for his services; the season would soon begin. Warner's choice for Jim would have been Cincinnati, but the world champion New York Giants offered Jim nearly $5,000 for one year. Jim sat in manager John J. "Muggsy" McGraw's office on February 1, 1913, and signed the agreement that would soon result in an unhappy alliance.

Although he suited up for every Giants game and traveled with the team, Jim only played in half a dozen games that summer. He felt almost as he had when he'd first joined the Carlisle team and was relegated to the bench. But this time there was no reason for it. Jim felt that his skills were being belittled and that the Giants had only wanted his name to attract fans to the games.

It seemed that there was a terrible impasse to some of those who were close to Jim and the Giants manager. McGraw claimed he couldn't let Thorpe play more often because Jim lacked hitting skills. Thorpe, on the other hand, claimed he had the skills but that when he stood at the plate, McGraw's constant sideline instructions about when to hit and where were unsettling.

Members of the team often told stories about how Thorpe and McGraw couldn't seem to get along and were always at each other's throats, sometimes almost coming to blows.

One bright spot in Jim's life, however, was Iva Miller, whom he had first met and dated when they were enrolled at Carlisle. Beautiful, bright, and witty, Scots-Irish-Cherokee Iva was extremely sensitive to Jim's feelings and offered the understanding he needed as he tried to realign his life.

At the end of baseball season, in October 1913, Jim and Iva were married in the Catholic church in Carlisle. A goodwill trip around the world with other team members and their wives served as Jim and Iva's honeymoon.

Upon their return to the United States, Jim and Iva settled into an apartment in New York City near the Polo Grounds where the Giants' home games were played. Iva, keenly interested in Jim's happiness, fit herself into his sports world. She attended the Giant games, both at home and away.

On May 8, 1915, a totally enchanted Jim Thorpe became the father of a son. Named James Francis, Jr., the baby brought great joy to the Thorpe household. Much of Jim's leisure time was spent beaming as he carried the child around, talking to and about him. As the baby grew, he seemed to have inherited much of Thorpe's fun-loving ways, enjoying their playful rough-and-tumble little games while Iva watched and laughed at their antics.

Meanwhile, earth-shaking events were changing the world. World War I had begun in 1914. In 1917 the United States entered the war, sending American boys abroad into a conflict which would continue into the next year.

Jim Thorpe's life was changing, too. When he had left the Carlisle Indian School to go into professional baseball, he had thought his football playing days were over. He never dreamed that professional football was in the wings.

In its infancy, it was not drawing the amount of enthusiastic fans that crowded baseball stadiums during the summer months. However, Jack Cusack, manager of the Canton Bulldogs football team, foresaw a greater future for the game. It

Jim Thorpe holding James Francis, Jr. (Photo courtesy of Oklahoma Historical Society, Archives and Manuscripts Division, Oklahoma City, Oklahoma)

was Cusack who approached Jim with the idea of joining the Bulldogs in his "spare time," especially since baseball and football seasons did not often overlap. The price he offered per game was not something Thorpe could afford to pass up.

And of course, Thorpe's love of the game had never diminished, so he happily got back into his favorite sport.

About this time, Jim, Iva, and Jim, Jr. moved back to Oklahoma. Jim was on the road so much it had become impossible for Iva to continue trying to attend all his games.

In 1917 their first daughter, Gail, was born. Once again, Jim was the ecstatic father.

But it seemed that Jim's life was destined for another cruel turn. Tragedy once again caught Jim in its unrelenting grasp when three-year-old Jim, Jr. was stricken with a serious influenza-like illness and died. Friends, teammates, and Iva all watched helplessly as Jim hit the skids again. Each family death in the past had devastated Jim, but the loss of his young son was the hardest blow he had ever had to bear. He began drinking more heavily and was dour and withdrawn whenever duties called him back to the football or baseball field.

His career with the Giants came to a vicious end when Giants manager McGraw spat out the wrathful remark that Jim was just a "dumb Indian." Thorpe had endured McGraw's domineering, blunt put-downs from the time he signed on with the Giants, often feeling that the remarks were uncalled for. But he could not, would not, allow McGraw to demean his Indian heritage. It took several team members to get the situation under control and keep blows from being struck.

Jim was almost immediately shipped off to the Boston Braves. He played for them until 1919.

CHAPTER 12

A Bridge to Build

By mid-September 1920, enough well-paying professional football teams had appeared on the scene for the owners to form a league. The American Professional Football League was established and Jim Thorpe was immediately proposed as its first president. In future years the league would be known as the NFL, or the National Football League.

Meanwhile, in the years after their young son's death, Iva had presented Jim with two more beautiful daughters: Charlotte and Grace. Jim was still the doting father although family life had become difficult to fit into his schedule. Between the games Jim still played in occasionally, appearances he had to make as president of the league, and socializing, Iva and Jim's home life was rapidly being destroyed. With three young children, Iva was no longer able to accompany Jim as she once had so enthusiastically, and they began to grow apart. In 1923, unable to reconcile the differences, they divorced.

In 1925 Thorpe married Freeda Kirkpatrick, a young lady from Ohio. He fathered four more sons: Carl Philip, William, Richard, and John. Once again, Jim was given the opportunity for a happy family life.

As he neared the age of forty, Jim began to recognize the inevitable signs of slowing. In 1928 he reluctantly retired from baseball; he played his last pro football game in 1929.

With no background other than in sports, Jim found himself unqualified for most types of work. As a result, he was usually offered only the most menial, low-paying jobs. With the Great Depression on, Thorpe found that what little he remembered from his carpentry and tailoring lessons at Carlisle did not hold him in good stead as he tried to provide food and shelter for his family.

There seemed to be some sunshine on the horizon when Metro-Goldwyn-Mayer bought the movie rights to Jim's life story. With Freeda and the boys, Jim moved to California to supervise the script and perhaps play a small part in the movie.

But after months of deliberation, it became clear that the story would not be filmed. The Thorpes found themselves stranded halfway across the country from their Oklahoma home, family, and friends. Jim was sometimes able to secure Indian bit parts in Westerns. But more often than not he was reduced to menial jobs calling for manual labor, which was often just plain ditch-digging.

In 1932, with the Olympic Games scheduled for Los Angeles, Thorpe's name and the history of his past Olympic greatness suddenly became newsworthy again. He found himself invited to sit with dignitaries at the opening of the Games. But although he was anxious to be there to cheer the athletes on, a news item reported that the "world's greatest athlete" couldn't afford the price of the ticket to the event. Through the generosity of those who remembered and still revered Jim Thorpe's Olympic saga, he was able to attend.

His name once more in the public eye, he was again sought for club appearances and speaking engagements. But his generous heart led him to appear without compensation, so his indebtedness increased.

On the speaking circuit, telling of his own athletic background, Jim entreated everyone to do their best at whatever they hoped to accomplish. He especially hoped to encourage youngsters in their dreams for the future. Requests for his appearances grew and soon he was traveling broader areas.

Often wearing his Native American garments to speaking engagements, Jim would explain their tradition and speak proudly of his Indian heritage. Through the years he had joined with others of his race to take a firm stand against the Bureau of Indian Affairs. He vigorously campaigned to Congress to abolish the bureau and let the Indians manage their own affairs, but the bill he represented was defeated.

The many appearances often entailed travel, once again separating Jim from home and family. This occurred to such an extent that in 1941 Freeda finally sued for divorce, citing not only his frequent prolonged absences but also his excesses in drinking.

World War II began late in 1941 and although Thorpe realized that at fifty-three he was much too old for the Army, he wanted to offer his services. A friend, aware of Thorpe's ambition, referred him to a former automobile manufacturing plant in Dearborn, Michigan, which now manufactured military vehicles. Thorpe's application was rewarded with a job. But a few months later Thorpe collapsed, suffering a heart attack.

Recovered enough for discharge from the hospital, he took his young sons and returned to Oklahoma to recuperate.

Enrolling the boys in the school there brought back painful memories of how much Jim had disliked school at their age. He especially remembered how his father had tried to impress upon him the necessity for education. Now he passed along the same words to his own sons.

Back on the family farm, with the boys in school, Thorpe hastened his recovery by retiring to the wilds with his hunting dogs and enjoying the serenity he had always found outdoors.

CHAPTER 13

The New Force in His Life

The year was 1945. The United States had been at war since December 7, 1941. During those four years, Thorpe had been advised numerous times that he was too old for service in any of the armed forces, but he had pursued his quest, feeling he should be lending support to his country.

Early that spring Jim married again. He took Patricia Askew from Louisville, Kentucky, for his third wife. As fate would have it, Jim had actually met Patricia some years before. The second time around, friendship blossomed into love.

Patricia was an able, take-charge person. She was determined from the start to put Thorpe's life on, if not a shining path, at least a straight one. She became his manager, orchestrating his speaking engagements and making certain he was now compensated for each one. This was definitely new for Thorpe, who was accustomed to saying yes when asked to do anything for anyone, anywhere, without reward. For the first time in years it seemed that he might be able to meet his bills. Meanwhile, Jim and Patricia lived frugally.

Then, just as their new life together seemed headed for solid ground, they were separated. Jim was called up by the branch of service he had applied to before his marriage. The merchant marine signed him on as a carpenter aboard the SS *Southwest Victory*, an ammunition/supply ship headed for the

Indian Ocean. Patricia, though shocked at the turn of events, proudly saw her husband off.

Although Jim was a mere carpenter, his past fame somehow became known on board and he was often called upon by the commandant to speak at military functions. Thorpe spoke of his athletic past, and as always, touched proudly upon his heritage.

The war ended shortly after the ship's return to home base and Jim was able to return to Patricia's side. Soon he was back to entertaining again, traveling about the area and on longer trips, to speak to schools and clubs. All of the events were coordinated through his wife.

Jim found a special joy in speaking to youth groups. He hoped to encourage them. Afterwards he sometimes jogged around the school yard or football field, the squealing, delighted children following in his footsteps.

Once again the idea of making a movie of Jim's life was probed. Metro-Goldwyn-Mayer still owned the rights, but in 1949 they agreed to sell the idea to Warner Bros., who promptly hired Thorpe as a consultant. He was also asked to train Burt Lancaster, who would be portraying Thorpe in the movie.

Meanwhile, in a poll of sportswriters and broadcasters, Jim Thorpe was named "the greatest football player of the first half century." This honor was followed shortly by another poll in which Thorpe was named the "best male athlete of the half century," surpassing even Babe Ruth, Jack Dempsey, and Ty Cobb.

With news of the honors reaching sports fans all over the world, Thorpe was sought after more and more. He was asked not only to deliver speeches, but also to receive more and more honors.

The movie of his life, *Jim Thorpe, All American,* was finally ready for release. Plans were made for dual premieres to be held on August 23, 1951, in Oklahoma City and Carlisle, Pennsylvania.

Dedication of Thorpe monument in Carlisle Square in 1951 (Photo courtesy of Cumberland County Historical Society, Carlisle, Pennsylvania 17013)

To coordinate with the opening of the movie, Carlisle dedicated a stone monument to Jim at the school. The ceremony was attended by numerous Pennsylvania officials as well as Phyllis Thaxter, who had portrayed Thorpe's wife Iva in the movie. Thorpe's eldest son, Carl Philip, unveiled the stone. Thorpe's eyes filled with tears as the inscription was read aloud:

> In recognition of the athletic achievements of Jim Thorpe, student of the Carlisle Indian School, Olympic champion at Stockholm in 1912, and in 1950 voted the greatest athlete and football player of the first half of the 20th century.

A few months later, the Thorpes' financial situation became embarrassingly public when Jim was hospitalized to have surgery on a cancerous growth on his lip. Despite all of Patricia's efforts, they had been unable to totally overcome Jim's indebtedness. The hospital listed Thorpe's name as a charity patient and the press leapt onto the news.

Shortly afterward, at home in Lomita, California, Jim suffered another heart attack. This time he did not survive.

Jim Thorpe died on March 28, 1953.

CHAPTER 14

A Legend Mourned

The next morning a stunned world heard the news of Jim Thorpe's death.

Forty years earlier, the young American Indian from Oklahoma had won the hearts of the world with his spectacular athletic feats in the 1912 Olympics.

A year later his fans had watched sympathetically as his heroics were stricken from the Olympic records.

Jim's athletic prowess, however, was not diminished, and he had gone on to further achievements in professional baseball and football. With the passing of the years, Thorpe, unwilling to give less than his best, had surrendered to age and left the field to a new generation.

Financial fate had seldom been kind to him, and when it was, his big heart had always shared with others. He was almost destitute when he died in Lomita, California, that day in 1953.

Thorpe lay in state while thousands filed past, paying last respects. He wore beaded moccasins on his feet and buckskin garments like those he had worn to speaking engagements. Among the many visitors were former teammates from the 1912 United States Olympic team, from the old New York Giants team, and from the Carlisle Indians. There were also old friends such as Gus Welch, who had served as best man when Thorpe married Iva Miller.

Patricia received condolences from all over the world, including a touching message from President Dwight D. Eisenhower, that young cadet who had played halfback for West Point in a game against the Carlisle Indians so long ago and still felt that "there was no one like him in the world!"

The Sac and Fox Indian tribe from Oklahoma was especially interested in seeing Thorpe returned to his native area for burial. Patricia, still trying to orchestrate finances as well as a suitable burial for him, agreed to have his body returned to Oklahoma. He was to be buried in Shawnee, in a mausoleum dedicated to his memory. A Roman Catholic funeral service was conducted and the body was held in a crypt. But when Patricia felt the memorial committee was not progressing quickly enough along the lines they had promised, she had the body moved to Tulsa to await a more definite decision.

About that time she heard the story of two small side-by-side towns in Pennsylvania that were experiencing financial as well as civic difficulties. Her astute mind sensed a solution that might work to her benefit as well as theirs. She made the trip east to the little town of Mauch Chunk (pronounced Mock Chunk, it's Indian for "sleeping bear") and sought a local spokesperson.

It was Joe Boyle whom Thorpe's widow first approached with her idea. Boyle, she had learned, was the ever-crusading editor of the Mauch Chunk *Times-News*. He had organized campaigns to revitalize the towns. One effort he had designed was the Nickel-A-Week Fund, which took a small amount from each resident for a nest egg for each town.

It might be beneficial to both towns, Patricia suggested to Boyle, to unite and benefit monetarily from tourism by using the name of a well-known person as a drawing card. By that, she meant, consolidate the two towns, change their names from Mauch Chunk and East Mauch Chunk to Jim Thorpe, and bury the legend there in a proper memorial, to be donated by the towns.

At first, Boyle had no intention of even considering Patricia's idea. But after mulling it over he saw merit in her plan. Certainly Jim Thorpe's name, his story, could be a drawing card, as she had suggested. Her offer of Thorpe's body, properly laid to rest in a beautiful mausoleum, would bring tourists who could jump-start the local economy.

Negotiations between the towns were worked out. They agreed to unite, change their names, and present a suitable mausoleum.

On Memorial Day, 1957, a beautiful, twenty-thousand-pound, red granite monument was completed and Jim Thorpe was finally laid to rest.

CHAPTER 15

Jim Thorpe, the Town

The area that is named for "the world's greatest athlete" has an interesting history.

One hundred years before, with its meandering river and spectacular Glen Onoko Falls, it had been known as the "Switzerland of America," running a close second to Niagara Falls as the honeymoon capital of the world.

Originally, the two little towns—Mauch Chunk and East Mauch Chunk—nestled side-by-side among mountains along the southern tip of the Poconos. Not much is remembered today about the reason for the enmity that once separated the towns.

What history does happily record, however, is the period in the late 1820s when Mauch Chunk and its neighbor formed a booming transportation center. Anthracite coal, at that time the principal source of energy and heat, was mined just to the north and was carted through Mauch Chunk on its way to heat the nation.

Josiah White, a major builder in the area along with George Hauto and Erskine Hazard, planned the creation of a port to which mined coal could be brought for shipment to Philadelphia. White was the inventor of the system of locks and dams which permitted the Lehigh River to become the first navigable river in the United States. With the invention of the switchback railroad, a gravity-rail system built in 1827, the "black gold" could be hastened out of the Lehigh Valley and into ports like Philadelphia and New York.

Men who had invested in and made millions from coal were entranced by the area's natural beauty and quickly adopted the lovely little towns, moving their families in with such vigor that there were soon known to be thirteen millionaires ensconced along the main street of Mauch Chunk.

Among them was Asa Packer, founder and president of the Lehigh Valley Railroad. A presidential candidate in 1868 and founder of Lehigh University, he was a generous philanthropist, always donating huge amounts to charitable organizations. He imported artisans and craftsmen all the way from Europe to Mauch Chunk in the 1860s to construct an elegant home for his wife and himself. The couple celebrated their golden wedding anniversary there in 1878. Known as the Asa Packer Mansion, the home still stands today.

In the Packer's library is a desk, chair, and bookcase once owned by General Robert E. Lee. The music room contains a fabulously beautiful crystal chandelier, a copy of which was used in used in the making of the movie *Gone With The Wind*. Throughout the house are exquisite marble pieces, fine crystal and china, beautiful sculptures, richly carved walnut furniture, and collections of beautiful paintings. In 1913, the house was donated to the town of Mauch Chunk by the Packers' daughter.

Mauch Chunk drew other fabled names, too. John Jacob Astor and his bride chose Mauch Chunk as their honeymoon site. President Theodore Roosevelt returned more than once and spoke glowingly of it. Several other presidents also spent time there. The towns were in their heyday.

Then suddenly petroleum replaced coal as the major fuel source. Coal was no longer referred to as "black gold." The once-burgeoning industry faltered, faded, and failed. By the late 1920s the millionaires had disappeared.

Mauch Chunk and East Mauch Chunk sank into a long-lasting, severe depression.

The arrival of Jim Thorpe's widow, Patricia, as she sought a burial place for the legend after his death in 1953, was looked upon with little interest by either town at first. However, when she touted the tourism that such a memorial would bring, townspeople listened to her proposal.

"Chunkers" on both sides of the river had begun to hear bits of gossip regarding the possibilities if the towns consolidated. One day there was a hint that a new hospital might be built in the town, bearing Jim Thorpe's name; a day later came more idle chatter that the Pro Football Hall of Fame might plan to move into the town; and so on.

After much deliberation, on May of 1954 the two towns voted to consolidate.

Jim Thorpe, Pennsylvania, not only survived, it thrived. Today, and for many years, the town of Jim Thorpe has happily borne the signs of affluence. Weekends find throngs of tourists as well as locals strolling about and sightseeing. The town's long, winding streets lead past intriguing little shops where casual friendliness seems the order of the day. Each season of the year is another drawing card. History abounds on all sides.

And here, visitors can pay their respects to the man for whom the town was named. At the edge of town, just off Route 903, is the beautiful twenty-ton red granite mausoleum, dedicated on Memorial Day, 1957. The memorial sits back from the road on a quiet, pretty, grassy knoll, just inside a circular drive. It bears the year of Thorpe's birth (1888) and his death (1953), with etchings depicting athletic events in his life. Inscribed are the words spoken so eloquently by King Gustav of Sweden as he presented the gold medals Jim Thorpe had won in the 1912 Olympics for the pentathlon and decathlon:

"Sir, you are the greatest athlete in the world."

Jim Thorpe's mausoleum (Photo courtesy of Delbert Updyke)

CHAPTER 16

Epilogue:
Gone But Not Forgotten

Honors for Jim Thorpe did not end with his death in 1953. An icon of his time, he continued to be remembered with awards from far and wide.

In 1955 the National Football League named its annual Most Valuable Player award "The Jim Thorpe Trophy."

1958 saw Thorpe being elected to the National Indian Football Hall of Fame in Anadarko, Oklahoma.

In 1961 he was named to the Pennsylvania Hall of Fame.

In 1963 he was inducted as a charter member of the Pro Football Hall of Fame in Canton, Ohio, where a life-sized statue of Thorpe stands in a prestigious spot near the front door.

In 1984 the U.S. Postal Service honored him with the issuance of a commemorative stamp.

Family members, friends, and admirers from around the world continued to try to have Thorpe's medals from the 1912 Olympics restored, but disappointment followed disappointment.

In October 1973, twenty years after Jim Thorpe's death, the Amateur Athletic Union finally agreed to the restoration of his amateur standing at the time of the 1912 Olympics. Two years later, the U.S. Olympic Committee, at the urging of its president William Simon, also endorsed the reinstatement

Statue of Thorpe located at Pro Football Hall of Fame, Canton, Ohio
(Photo courtesy of Cumberland County Historical Society,
Carlisle, Pennsylvania 17013)

of Thorpe. The International Olympic Committee, however, remained adamant in their stand.

It was not until October 1982, after meeting with Simon, that the new IOC president Juan Antonio Samaranch proposed restoration of Thorpe's amateur status. The move, however, only allowed Thorpe's name to be added to the record books as "co-champion" along with the second- and third-place finishers Wieslander and Bie.

Charlotte Thorpe, one of Iva Miller and Jim Thorpe's daughters, supported the co-champion agreement. "It would have been morally unjust," she considered, "to strike their [Wieslander and Bie] names and restore the sole winner of the decathlon/pentathlon as one James Francis Thorpe." She applauded Samaranch's efforts.

On January 18, 1983, the IOC issued duplicate medals to Thorpe's children. Now the family hopefully awaits the day that the trophies that were presented to Thorpe will also be returned.

Now, almost fifty years after Thorpe's mausoleum was dedicated, students at Carbon County Area Vocational-Technical School are working on upgrading and beautifying the memorial. A preliminary design for the work included the installation of concrete walkways, a driveway to arc the mausoleum, lights, flagpoles, a memorial sign marker, and informational signs, as well as landscaping. Work on the project continues to enhance tourism in the lovely little town of Jim Thorpe, as visitors come to pay their respects to the unforgettable athlete.

*Bill Thorpe, Jr., a grandson of Jim Thorpe, and Gina Hemphill, grad-
daughter of Jesse Owens, another Olympic champion, carrying the Olympic
torch upon its arrival in New York, on its way to the 1984 Olympic Games
in Los Angeles* (Photo courtesy of UPI/Corbis-Bettman)

This poem was written by Jim Thorpe's daughter, Charlotte, in remembrance of her father's loss of his twin brother and best friend, Charley, at the age of eight.

Lost Brother in the Wind

by Charlotte Thorpe

The Earth people called him
    Wa-Tha-Huck,
His skin gleamed with a
    ruddy glow.
He was an Indian youth
    and he ran across fields,
        he jumped fences
    and he shunned "things below."
His vision came from above.
His pleasure was running
        wild and free
    from field to forest . . . he ran.
Crossing waters whose currents
    were strong.
He was free, and,
    he could do no wrong.

He put together a ball
    filled it with dried leaves and twigs.
He stuffed these into
    stocking material
    and he threw it into the air . . .
    he had made a ball.

He threw his ball to his twin
    brother, Charley.

Charley looked at the ball,
        looked at Jim,
        smiled . . . and,
        kicked the hand-made
ball that was stuffed with
        leaves and twigs.

Wa-Tha-Huck caught the small ball
        made a lunge at Charley
                who ducked playfully.
Then Jim ran fast with the ball
                tucked under one arm . . .

He brushed a bush, he jumped a
        felled log,
He jumped another fence
        his father had made.
He shouted, "Catch me, Charley . . .
        see if you can catch me."
Wa-Tha-Huck glanced back at Charley
        who stood woefully still
"I can't catch you, Jim . . .
                you're too fast
                        as fast as a horse . . .
'sides, I don't feel good, Jim.
                        I'm going home."

Charley went home
        Their mother held him close,
tending his feverish body.
That night . . . Charley died.
Jim cried
                he sighed
                he moaned, and
                he groaned.
His heart ached for his brother
        who was growing cold.

Who will I play with now
        wondered Wa-Tha-Huck?
Who will I wrestle with?
Who will catch my ball?
Will the wind carry my ball
        to Charley?
Will he see me in the fields?

That's *our* eagle that just
        flew over . . .
dipping one wing
        and then the other . . .
then, soaring higher
        ever higher.
That's *our* eagle, thought Jim
        mine and Charley's.
I'll watch for *our* eagle every day
        and Charley will see it too . . .
        I *know* he will.

Charley really didn't leave me
        he's flying with *our* eagle.
Oh, I wish I could fly
        with *our* eagle
        and Charley.
I want to be with them.

I guess I'll just run some more . . .
I'll run and, I'll jump . . .
I'll throw the ball to the wind,
        but, Jim didn't run so gleefully
Jim didn't jump so high . . .
        he couldn't
Charley made his heart too heavy.

But in 1912, Jim ran . . . Jim jumped
he put the shot . . .
he threw the javelin . . .
Charley ran with him, and *their* eagle
flew over Mount Olympus!

Charlotte Thorpe with her father's memorabilia (Courtesy of Charlotte Thorpe)

Further Suggested Reading

Bernotas, Bob. *Jim Thorpe, Sac and Fox Athlete.* New York and Philadelphia: Chelsea House Publishers, 1992.

Carbon County Tourist Promotion Agency. *Jim Thorpe, the Man and the Town.*

Carlson, Lewis H., and Fogarty, John J. *Tales of Gold.* Chicago/New York: Contemporary Books.

Coffey, Wayne. *Jim Thorpe, Olympic Gold.* Boulder: Black Birch Press, Inc., 1992.

D'O'Brian, Joseph. "The Greatest Athlete in the World." *Heritage Magazine* (July/August 1992).

Gobrecht, William. *Jim Thorpe, Carlisle Indian.* Camp Hill: Continental Press, 1969.

Knight, Theodore. *The Olympic Games.* San Diego: Lucent Overview Series, 1991.

Nardo, Don. *The Importance of Jim Thorpe.* San Diego: Lucent Books, 1944.

Newcombe, Jack. *The Best of the Athletic Boys.* Garden City: Doubleday & Co., 1975.

Richards, Gregory B. *Jim Thorpe, World's Greatest Athlete.* Chicago: Children's Press, 1984.

Santrey, Lawrence. *Jim Thorpe, Young Athlete.* Mahwah: Troll Associates, 1983.

Schoor, Gene (with Henry Gilford). *The Jim Thorpe Story.* New York: Archway Paperback Pocketbook, 1951.

Wallenchinsky, David. *The Complete Book of the Olympics.* New York: Penguin Books, 1984.

Wheeler, Robert W. *Jim Thorpe, World's Greatest Athlete.* Norman: University of Oklahoma Press, 1978.